KAYCEE MARLETT

Be Real In Your Budget

The content of this book is intended for informational purposes only. Information compiled, specifically regarding bankruptcy, may or may not reflect the most current developments. You are advised to follow federal, state and local government laws and directives. The author disclaims any personal liability, loss or risk incurred as a result of the use of any information or advice contained in this book, either directly or indirectly.

Dedication

I want thank my Mom and Dad who insisted that I balance my finances and never live beyond my means, who taught me to save for the rainy days that come, to look for the rainbows of life and the promises that it holds.

I am grateful to the following people who without their help and direction this book would not have ever got beyond the computer upon which it was typed.

To my dear friend Michele who is always an encouragement to me to reach for the unreachable stars. For working together to ensure that we could reach toward the goal of supplying Lifeline Ministry; enabling it to bring smiles to children at Christmas with the toys we have been able to supply to them; preparing and delivering the Thanksgiving meals to those who just needed a helping hand; for the past and future supplying of much needed items of food and shelter of those who are struck by disaster.

To JennIfer for lending her talent of proofreading to ensure that all the "t's" were crossed and the "i's" dotted.

To Danielle for sharing her amazing creative ability

with graphics and designing the cover.

I want to thank God for giving me the drive to write this book to help others. The simplicity of the book and the content, are great tools to anyone who wants to trim their budget or work out the bugs it may have.

Preface

HOOK LINE AND SINKER was written for the average person who may be sitting at their kitchen table; hand in their hair, wondering how to stop the downward spiral of debt while they attempt to make ends meet. This book stands apart from the other budgeting and money management books on the shelves as it contains practical, easy to apply tips that can be done **now**. No college degree, financial planner, personal banker or fancy software needed – not that those things aren't valued and great – but they are not necessary to put these tools to work **today**.

Managing a workable budget takes wisdom, not a fly by the seat of your pants balancing act. Wisdom is not complicated, intricate or unobtainable – wisdom is **founded on Truth**. Although it may be enticing to look for a get rich quick scheme, simple and consistent steps that lead you out of debt will get you further down the road on more stable ground.

Implementing simple tools into your budget, keeping track of your spending and staying focused on the goals that you will set, will be your success. No great fish story about how your budget got away from you to tell! Instead, you will reel in the stress of an overweight budget, allowing you to get a proper picture of a balanced budget.

Get a hook into your finances; don't let it get away from you. You are your best and worst enemy when it comes to managing your money. Sink your debt, before it sinks you!

Table of Contents

Introduction

When I set out to write this book I wanted to share the little things that make a budget work. There are many other books written on budget making, and how to create a budget. But in many cases I have found that they are not written for the everyday "Joe".

The simplicity of budgeting has been, in my opinion, blown completely out of proportion. Making the idea of a balanced budget seemingly unreachable, it is attainable. Is creating and living within a balanced budget easy? The answer is, it can be, with some work and self determination, which rises from you, disciplining you.

Likened unto exercise, the body will respond with a few muscles groaning and aching, when one begins to put a demand their body. After 30 days of exercise you begin to see a change. We all want to have well shaped bodies, healthy and youthful if not in years then at least in performance.

Along with exercise, you must change the way you eat to attain the results that you are striving toward. A budget is the same as a diet. It takes a decision, determination, and goal orientation, but you'll love the results.

Also compared to a person who has decided to go on a healthy life changing diet, many people even those who love you can become a stumbling block when you decide to change you. Don't let them. Your success is not based on their failures, or your past failures. Your success is based on you making a decision today and sticking to your goal, not someone else's opinion or comments.

I hope that you enjoy this tool, in balancing your budget. It is one tool, a useful one, yet as time goes by you will be adding more tools to your arsenal to stay the path and keep to your goal.

I once heard that a study was done at a renowned University, that after twenty years the results were in, of a class of 100 persons it was determined that 92% of the people in the class did not have any set goals, ideas but not goals. Another 6% had goals, knew the direction they were going to pursue, yet still they did not write down their goals. The remaining 2% of the class had written their goals down, kept them with them throughout the days. Of the entire class that was reassembled some twenty years later, it was found that those of the 92% who never had goals were like so many people we see today drifting from one thing to the next; the group of 6% who had goals in mind but did not write them down were found to be above average in success, yet still found themselves not where they thought they would be; the third group, the group of 2% who had written their goals, read them and kept them, were discovered to have exceeded their original goals and had added to them over the years, surpassing their original intent.

Because you are reading this book, you have decided to balance your budget. This is a great tool to start with, but not as important as the pen and paper you will be using to write down your goals. As you learn valuable information on budgeting, write down those things that apply to you. Make your way through your list and you will see results.

One day at a time, will soon add up to be a week, then a month. As a year passes you will see your own personal wealth and well being materializing in your life. Stick to your goals you will have mapped yourself success.

Personally, I have created new businesses and have also successfully run businesses for others. I could not and would not have been successful in any of the ventures I have been a part of with out first knowing what the goal of the business was to pursue. Writing down goals, creating a "to do list", attributed to each success. Honestly, the businesses that I have also been a part of that failed were based upon the fact there was no plan to succeed, nothing written down just a bunch of talk, no commitment.

When you write your goals down, you are making a commitment to yourself. Keep your word, follow the plan, you will succeed.

The old saying "That if you fail to plan, you plan to fail", holds true in business financing and personal finances.

1 - What Is a Budget?

Everyone has a budget. You may not live by rules that say you are living with a budget, but you are. Just because you have no parameters that you live within doesn't mean that you do not have a budget. It does mean that you have no guidelines, restraints, or boundaries. The idea that someone may say that they have no need to budget, makes as much sense as the person who feels they have no need to diet.

Allow the following idea to play out; if you eat anything, you are on a diet, if you don't eat anything, you are on a diet. Same goes for a budget. You could have a balanced diet, be slightly under or over weight, be bulimic, obese, or anorexic, these are all diets. When it comes to your budget it can be just like one of these diets.

A balanced budget is one that has taken into account the needs of the household, personal needs, and future needs while constantly working out the bugs to ensure a healthy outcome.

A budget that is slightly over weight is a budget that has very few flings of spending. Usually with this budget type the "**flings**" are seemingly slight, not really over doing or spending in one area, but a few indulges that keep the budget off balance.

A **bulimic budget** has within its parameters ups and downs - spending sprees with regrets, sometimes returning items that were later determined not needed or over spending then not spending, for basic needs like housing and necessities, because there is no money to pay for them.

An **obese budget** is one that is just too much in all areas. From the wasting of electricity, to gluttonous waste of spending on useless and unneeded items that are tossed about in closets, cupboards, shelving, never to be used, forgot about until one moves or one sees one of those remarkable home makeovers, or spring cleaning to clean out that "extra junk"; only to find themselves in the same predicament in the future as the behavior has not changed.

The **anorexic budget** is as deadly as the eating disease that it is named after. Scrooge, the classic Christmas Carol story, is an excellent example of this type of budget mindedness, better known as "extreme penny pinching."

In the opening act, it begins with a fear of not having enough coal to heat the room. It is a great depiction of how some people will take frugality to an unhealthy level. Frugally maintaining your needs when economic times demands it takes discipline to ensure survival. However, when it is taken to extremes, to where you live so far beneath your means to ensure that your bank account grows, it becomes unhealthy. You will eventually starve yourself of some of the very basic needs that will ensure a sound life that instead, dies and withers due to lack of proper care.

Living Beyond Your Income Stream

Spending beyond your income is dangerous. If you find that you do, you're in good company. The United States Government figures show that many households with a total income of $50,000 or less are currently spending more than they bring in. Without proper budget alignment, foreclosure, vehicle repossession, and poor credit ratings will soon follow. Today's volatile economy reeks with uncertainty. With unstable economics, from countries to citizens, the cascading of failed economies is toppling down on the masses, but not on all individuals, the tumult is creating a dismal news cast. However, you do not have to participate, nor be a martyr for the current events that's taking place today! All you have to do is manage your own space and life. If you do, and as others begin their endeavor to balance their lives and budget, the economy will right itself over time. But change has to happen, and it does start with you.

If you make ten dollars an hour, then live like you make 6 dollars per hour, don't max out your spending. Why? It is simple really, to become debt free. The odds are that you are in debt of some respect. Maybe it's a car loan, credit cards or check advance services.   Incidentally, those businesses have an average of 30% or greater interest rate, to name a few.

You can dig yourself out. You are capable of financial freedom no matter where you start from, as long as you start, keep your eye on the goal and you will bury your debt.

With the money you do not spend, after you have set aside your savings, you need to pay down one debt at a time. Your accumulation of debt did not come on one occasion; it came one debt at a time.

Pulling in the Reins on Spending

Now that you have been made aware that your spending is out of balance, you need to take some time to analyze your assets, costs and debt. Once you begin to evaluate yourself and your household, do not become dismayed and think that you will not be able to make adjustments to bring your budget into a healthy balance, you can and you will.

However, don't over analyze. You will find you will become overwhelmed and stultified into a frozen state of doing nothing because you will believe that "NOTHING" can work or help.

If you are looking for instantaneous resolution or results, be prepared to be dismayed and watch as failure creeps in to win. In order to reach your goals of safe and comfortable financial living, you will need to have a disciplined (not tyrannical) approach. You must decide if your future is valuable to you. Do nothing and indeed you will fail! If you go on a crash diet of budgeting that too will fail. Be reasonable with yourself and your budget. It didn't become like it is overnight and it will not be healed and corrected overnight.

If you are dreaming of winning the lottery (who knows, you might) it is keynote to say that most, if not all, previous lottery winners have found themselves right back where they were (if not in more dire circumstances) prior to winning a large sum of money. Why? Because the budget habits before winning the monies were not healthy to begin with and the results of poor money management continue to be the same.

Teach yourself and learn how to be faithful with what you have - whether it is a small income or a large income. Take care of your money, be vigilant to rule it well, not be ruled by your circumstances and you will be able to manage more as you implement better savings plans and investments. If you have never ran a mile, or trained for running any long distance, what are the chances that you would be able to complete running mile on the spur of the moment? You have to train yourself to run just like you have to train yourself to save.

Setting Boundaries

Even if you are born into money there are boundaries, or in the case of money management, allowances. One of the first things that you must begin to assess is what are your **absolutes** and what are your **variables**. If you were asked what is the one thing that you could not live without; do you know what that one thing would be? Let's examine what could possibly be the one thing.

1.   place to live
2.   food to eat
3.   vehicle to drive
4.   utilities
5.   insurance
6.   gas for vehicle
7.   clothes to wear

So which one of the things stated above is your one thing? You could say that "all were important" or "most were important to me". You notice that you can have none of those things unless they are financially provided for. Even if you are in jail, it still takes financial support to provide housing, food and clothing. It can be stated then that none of those things listed above is the one thing. Indeed the one thing is your source of income.

Your source of income does establish your boundaries. You may stretch your boundaries but, like a rubber band you will snapped back into reality as any persons budget can be stretched to unreasonable lengths and finally give way.

Know yourself, know your boundaries and learn to live within your means. You may have to give up some things now to have a future. On this note every generation has thought they were the last one, and at different times have had these anomalies of spending and financial upheaval, spending their future as if there wasn't one.

In our recent history, we have rewritten mortgage rules to fit our now. I have got to have it now spending and committing to payments that we can not afford has spent our future. Many persons are finding that they have spent so much of their future that cannot live now. You may even be one of these persons who find themselves within that predicament. If you are reading this ebook then at least you are researching how to get out of your mess now. The information in this ebook will help you, but you will have to use the information from here and possible other resources to complete your task.

Learning to Live Within Your Means of Support

When you decide to live within your income level, then you will be on the road to success. The decision will always be a life changing one. Why must it be life changing? Because you are taking steps to ensure your positive success it can be no less than life changing. In fact you will begin to see yourself as a person who truly has success based upon solid principles and not just lipstick and rouge that hides all of the flaws.

Imagine the less stress you will have in your life when you are no longer maintaining a house of cards, but a home built upon rock solid foundation. First evaluate your needs, then wants. Then assess what and how you are going to meet your needs. How you do this is simply done be asking yourself the following questions and answering them truthfully.

1. Do you have a solid career?

2. Do you need to have a supplement income to support yourself and your family?

3. Is there too much month at the end your money?

4. Are credit cards or check cashing stores your second income?

5. Are you on the revolving credit treadmill?

6. Does the thought of bankruptcy cross your mind?

7. Will a credit Counselor or services work for me?

8. Are you seeing foreclosure of your home in the near future?

9. Is there possibility of car repossession?

10. Will a chronic illness/accident wipe you out?

11. Is the rent you're paying too high for your income?

12. Are you struggling to buy the groceries you need for your home?

13. Is your money working for you or do you do all the work for the money?

When you can answer the above questions honestly and truthfully to yourself, then you are ready to address the changes that you need and follow through with the adjustments that you know must be done.

2 - Creating a Budget You Can Live With

When you begin to make a budget, the first thing you do is write down your list of needs in an order that evolves to your wants.

The A list

1. food
2. housing
3. utilities
4. vehicle
5. insurance
6. recreation
7. retirement
8. spending money

One of the easiest ways to set up your budget is to use software that will help you stay on track; like MS Money, or Quickbooks. However, just in case you haven't access to those great tools, the basic spiral notebook and pen will do. So pull up your boot straps, buckle up and keep your hands and feet in front you as proceed forward.

Food

One of the quickest ways to blow your budget is in the food category. Instantaneously, you summon up in your mind, your total spending that you have every time you go to the grocery store. But wait! The grocery store is not your only food bill. You need to look at where you are frivolously spending you money on food and beverage items. Just like any diet regime that you go on, the most crucial tool you can implement is the small notebook and pen.

When you use a notebook and pen that you keep on your person or within close reach, you can track your spending which seems too small to have to count. It is the little things that can lead to big the things. Remember, you are getting your budget within your reach. Relieve the undue stress from the weight of your obligations so don't give up, or become discouraged. You can and will get through this time.

Okay, now back to the notebook and pen. What you need to do with your new financial tools is, track your spending every day for the next 30 days. Be honest, you are helping yourself. You are not doing this for anyone else's benefit, this is for you. So, just like when you go on a "diet" know what you are consuming in a day, week and finally the month.

Let's do an example - you are on your way to work and you stop to get a quick $1.89 coffee everyday at the local convenient store. You are patting yourself on the back because you aren't stopping at Starbucks for the $4.00

latte. While you are in the convenience store, a well placed advertisement for a $1.00 breakfast sandwich with the purchase of your coffee, grabs your attention. Great! Now you have coffee and breakfast for the same price you were spending on a latte. Now you head off to work. While the morning rolls on, you find that you are getting a little hungry, but it isn't quite lunch time. So you stroll over to grab something to munch on from the snack machine and plug in 75 cents. You think you will eat half now and save half for later, after lunch. Now lunch rolls around and you pat yourself on the back because you have brought your lunch, but you need a drink. You revisit the vending area and buy yourself something to drink for $1.00. You plan to sip on it now and enjoy it for the next hour. As 3 p.m. rolls around, you decide to stretch a bit and take a break in the break room. There is a water fountain there and you get yourself a drink from it. As you start back to your desk you think, "Hmmm I'll just get myself a bottle of water for the rest of the day from the machine...I need some water" and off to vending machine you go, and out goes another $1.25. At the end of the day, you head home and you are happy with your day! You think of the things you need from the grocery store and stop in. You walk out of the store happy that you only spent $30.00 because it wasn't really your shopping day, you just wanted to get a few items to make it until then.

So let's see –

Example - daily

Item	Daily Cost	Over Time
Convenience store breakfast	$ 2.89	
Vending machine snack	0.75	
Vending machine drink	1.00	
Vending machine water	1.25	
totals	$ 5.89	$ 29.45 per week
		$132.53 per month
Extra grocery shopping	$30.00	
	avg. 2.2 times/week	$ 66.00 per week
		$297.00 per month

Let's also include the one time per week that you have set aside for yourself to go out to eat, which averages moderately around $16 per person. Let's say its date night, so for 2 people you budget $32 and don't forget to tip, so add another $7, making it $39.

Example - monthly

Item	Weekly Cost	Monthly Cost
Date night	$ 39.00	$175.50
Budgeted groceries	125.00	562.50
Daily convenience foods	29.45	132.53
Extra grocery shopping	66.00	297.00
Totals	**$259.45**	**$1,167.53**

Here Is an Alternative Scenario

You take a thermal cup of coffee with you, as well as the quick egg and toast sandwich you have made yourself to work with you in the morning. When mid morning comes around and you have a craving, you pull out of your lunch bag snack. It's more than likely more healthy and more reasonably costing than the vending machine item. It's also accommodated with the bottle water that you have brought with you. (Note unless the water from the drinking fountain that may be available to you is completely rancid, refill your bottle with that water for the afternoon.) At your lunch break you enjoy the drink you brought from home. Most businesses have a break room with some facilities, one usually being a refrigerator, microwave etc; if not the reliable thermos works very well to keep liquids cold or hot. For the afternoon, you refill your water bottle and eat your pre packed snack. When you are on your way home, you are thinking about your prepared menu for the evening you have created before you go to the grocery store, and purchased accordingly.

Example B – daily & monthly

Item	Daily Cost	Over Time
Packed snacks	$ 0.50	$ 2.50
Bottles of water	$ 0.25	1.25
Date night with coupon		18.00
Groceries with coupons		95.00
Totals	**$ 0.75 daily**	**$116.75 weekly**
		$525.38 monthly

Cost comparison

Item	Monthly Cost	Cost Difference
Example A spending	$1,167.53	
Example B spending	$ 525.38	
Savings		**$642.15 monthly**

So in our reasonable example you can see that with some planning you can begin to reach some of your financial goals. If you are already taking some of the saving steps listed above, include them all and add your own to increase your savings. If you have another great saving idea, feel free to post it on out blog, at www.inmyalley.com/blog .

Check out the coupon section in www.inmyalley.com for your printable and online coupons, as well as links to sites with the coupon codes that can save you money. There is also some great ideas and tips on how to control your grocery shopping purchases, along with some helpful buying tips and tricks with BOGO offers.

If you haven't read any of the great articles on coupon savings, there are some good ones for you to read and apply their methods to your budget to help you save lots of money.

Housing

Housing - this can be tough topic. If you are in an upside down mortgage, at the time of this writing the current President of the United States is President Obama, he and his staff are pounding out a bailout package that is supposed to help those who find themselves owing more than their property is worth. As the package is revealed and unfolded for the consumer we will have articles on this topic within www.inmyalley.com .

For the rest of us who can do something now

Let's be realistic, if you are falling behind in your mortgage there are some things that you can do right now that will help to you to climb out of your dilemma. **But you have to do something.** No one but you knows what is going on in your finances. If you are falling behind on your mortgage payments, **call your mortgage company**, using the customer service number on your statement. Banks don't want to take your home; they want you to keep it. Your mortgage company may be able to work with you or offer you some options, but they can't help you unless you call them. Set your pride aside and call. Avoiding the issue won't help you. Calling might!

By the news media's standard depiction, all around is financial crisis and failure. But you do not have to fall prey to the fear about you. So let's address how to tackle what you have in debt and what it takes for you to tread through this recession of time.

Let's organize your fixed spending. Note the numbers used below are for illustration purposes and are based on the National Average. We have added space for you to begin writing down your spending in these areas.

Housing costs:

Item	Nat'l Avg.	Your Amt.
Mortgage with Interest	$1,497.00	
Insurance average	112.50	
Property tax	234.00	
Total Monthly Mortgage Payment	$1,843.50	

Or perhaps you rent:

Item	Nat'l Avg.	Your Amt.
2 Bedroom/ 2 Bath	$1,250.00	

Utilities

Item	Nat'l Avg.	Your Amt.
Electricity**- before taxes and service fees	$ 173.40	
Natural gas	50.00	
Water/sewer	113.00	
Cable	98.00	
Telephone/Internet	103.00	
Cell phone – family average	211.00	
Total Monthly Utilities	$748.40	

**Electricity per kilowatt national avgerage 9.92 cents @ 1450 kilowatt usage

Vehicle

Item	Nat'l Avg.	Your Amt.
Vehicle Payment	$500.00	
Vehicle Insurance	140.00	
Fuel	162.00	
Maintenance	54.00	
Average Monthly Vehicle Cost	$856.00	

Insurance

Illustration based on a single person

Item	Nat'l Avg.	Your Amt.
Health Insurance	$250.00	
Life Insurance	44.00	
Short Term Insurance	90.00	
Average Monthly Insurance Cost	$536.50	

Recreation

Just like the other categories in your budget, you need to set aside money for recreation. If you don't, you may spend more than you have and dip into your essentials such as housing or food. As the economy falls, so does this monthly allowance. However, you should calculate a maximum amount designated for recreational use. Why? The answer is simple, if you do not have an allowance, your budget will seem too overwhelming and you may over indulge yourself.

The National Average Median Income per year, based on US Government statistics, is $40,342. If you consider that number with the current economic affairs, it would seem reasonable that you should not exceed more than 2.5% of your income to recreation.

This is also the category you can use to plan a future get-away or vacation. Carve out a few dollars every week from your recreation budget and put it into a vacation fund and start planning your vacation!

Item	Nat'l Avg.	Your Amt.
Monthly Recreation	$84.04	

Allowance for spending freely is also a neccesity; however the amount should be established and firmly adhered to, but **should not be based upon the available credit you have on your credit cards**.

Retirement

It is difficult to answer the question, "How do I save when there is nothing to left over to save." However, let's be totally clear; if you do not save even what seems trifle in these times, you will be destitute and penniless with no way to retire. Retirement will not be on your radar and you will be working till the day you die.

A standard rule to apply is, pay yourself 10% of your income. If you cannot do that now, the question is - how soon could you? Also, ask yourself this question "what does my future look like if I do <u>not</u> save now?" By the way, that is 10% of your <u>gross</u> not net income. So again, ask yourself, if not now, when? If you do not plan on your future, you essentially plan to fail.

Item	Nat'l Avg.	Your Amt.
Monthly Retirement	<u>$336.18</u>	

3 - Creative Steps to Take to Keep a Budget Balanced

When you have done all that you can do, and still keep all that you have, with the ability to save some for what could be called a hail storm and not a rainy day, then when the wolf comes calling, you need to assess your fixed spending as discussed in the last chapter to determine what you can cut.

For some, their budget will allow a little cut from everywhere. Take the example of negotiating with your services.

Insurance

Let's evaluate the cost of insurance. If you have been with the same company for several years, do some shopping around for other car insurance company quotes. You may find that your current company has been increasing rates with a very slow drain to your wallet. If that is the case, before you leave your company, call them and ask if they will match the price you have found that will better suit your wallet. Now bear in mind that you need to be completely honest with yourself when you make comparisons of insurance. All insurance company policies are not created equal. The differences for example may be comparing apples to oranges or of the quality of Outback Steak House to McDonalds. So checkout your comparison insurance shopping before you begin your negotiations.

Health Insurance

Shop and compare health insurance rates. You may have insurance through an employer – you may be surprised to find you can get the same coverage independently for less, especially if your coverage includes family members. If you have experienced health issues recently, now is likely not the time to switch carriers.

- Prescription cards can save you money

- Dental and Optical cards can reduce your costs with a small annual premium.

Life Insurance

Consider making your life insurance a part of your savings plan by investing in Whole Life.

If you are struggling to save money and pay for your life insurance you can combine long term savings that can be borrowed against, up to the amount that you have invested until its maturity date. Although a whole life premium is higher, it has a two-fold function; life insurance and a savings plan.

For example, let's say you can manage to save $50 a month and your life insurance plan is roughly $50, you can combine the two and use the $100 to purchase a whole life insurance policy and have both savings and life insurance.

Instead of carrying a higher premium life insurance, determine how much insurance you and your family really need at this time.

During an economic crisis one of the first things that people will give up is their life insurance. Before you give up on all life insurance plans consider what the cost of burial would add up to in cost for your family.

Another alternative to inquire about is to check if you can add a manageable life insurance plan through your bank that would be pennies on the day, instead of dollars a day.

Short Term Insurance

If you lose your income due to illness or injury, even in good economic times it can be a costly.

If you are considering dropping all your health and life insurance premiums, there are alternatives to meeting your needs. You need coverage, weigh the consequences, and look for alternatives.

One alternative that may meet all your short term needs is supplemental insurance, a product that can cover:

- Short term illness
- Death
- Accidents
- Income replacement
- Dental
- Vision

One company is American Income Life. It is one of several companies that offer an alternative that will work for you now and in the future. Consider the available offers that these companies offer and weigh out the cost savings that could be beneficial to you and your family.

Vehicle Insurance

As already stated above, **shop around** for a more cost efficient insurance policy. Also consider the monthly cost savings on your premium by **increasing your deductible**, if you are good driver. However, remember what you could afford to pay if you were to be without your vehicle for a few unfortunate repair days.

If you are not upside down on your vehicle and had opted for the **GAP** insurance when you purchased your vehicle, consider **canceling it**. It will save you a few dollars a month and you may receive a refund for what you have already paid in.

Mortgage Insurance

If you have been making all of your payments on your mortgage on time for at least 6 months, and now have paid down your principal so that it is under 80% of what the value of your home was at the time of your purchase or refinance, call your mortgage company and see if you can have the cost of the mortgage insurance removed from your payment.

Example: original loan amount $90,000, divided by value of the home at that time $100,000 = 90% loan to value. Now that you have been paying on your mortgage for some time, perhaps making extra principal payments as discussed above, your principal balance is $79,000 – this would bring your original loan to value down to 79%. In this example, if the market has declined and your home is no longer valued at $100,000 you may need to make yourself a note to check later. It is worth a call to your mortgage company to see if you can **drop your mortgage insurance**!

Home Services

Telephone services

If you have both a home phone service and cell phone service, determine your need for home service if you need a home phone, as an **alternative** to pricey long distance and local services are:

- **Magic Jack**- plugs into your USB port on your computer and then you plug you regular phone into the jack.

- **Vonage**- adapter plugs into computer.

- Your cable service may offer phone service at a lower cost.

Remember the idea is to reduce your cost of living, without sacrificing your needs.

Dish TV/ Direct TV/Cable/Air HD TV

Although both are comparable, their service prices range drastically. If one service offers "for new customers a great rate", **call your current provider** and ask for a discount, or simply reduce your charges by cutting back your package.

How much TV do you really watch? Decide if a **HDTV converter box** will suffice your needs. Most information you want from TV can be found on the internet and bridged to your flat screen TV.

There are movies that **you can watch online.** Find out more at www.yourinformationhighway.com. This site has many great tips on how to watch and where to find movies online. There are helpful links for downloadable as well as streaming movies for your entertainment pleasure.

Internet Providers

Not all Internets are created equal. Cable has its advantages as it has quick speed. Review your package and determine if you really do need the fastest speed, do you really need TURBO. What is your package cost? What does it include? Can you **trim it down**? Dial-up although it can be cost efficient it is not the most viable resource for internet usage. DSL Broadband- some phone companies provide DSL service as well and will allow you to have the DSL service without the cost of a home phone line as well. ATT offers this amenity.

When you are reviewing your internet and phone services, count the cost and the weigh it against your financial objectives. You will find that your penny savings, added to dimes and nickels will begin to add up to dollars.

Additional Savings

- Checkout the energy savings tips, at www.inmyalley.com to reduce your daily energy consumption and costs.

- Also look for the Fuel Savings ebook coming soon, that can help you save money while you are commuting to work as well as doing your errands.

4 - Curbing Your Interest Consumption

Interest on the average home mortgage will cost the homeowner nearly TWO TIMES the cost of the home. If you were to purchase a $150,000 home with a $120,000 mortgage (80%), and you paid an interest rate of 9% for 30 years, you will have paid over $227,500 just in interest (in addition to the original $120,000). That's nearly two times the cost of the home!

While you are addressing your monthly budget, it would be amiss to leave out costly credit cards. While the national average credit card debt owed per household is $7000, you must realize the real cost of what your credit cards are costing you.

A credit card debt of $7,000 (now the average) at 21% being paid at the rate of $25 principal plus interest each month will take over 29 YEARS to pay off, almost as long as a home mortgage. Interest charged on this credit card debt will top $21,400, more than 3 TIMES your original debt!

As you work for a living, you know that when you are not working, you are not getting paid. But interest never gets sick, never takes a vacation and never sleeps. It is working against you 24 hours a day, seven days a week, each and every day of the year, year in and year out.

So what can you do to pay down your debt?

You may not be able to pay off your debts or mortgage now, again if you could you would have done so and would not be seeking budget counseling now. You may not have enough equity in your home for a loan. You may not be able to afford the refinancing costs or home equity loan costs. You may not be able to lower your credit card interest rates.

But you can make additional or extra payments as you budget in the reduction of your debt.

So how does making an extra payment help lower your interest charges? Is it going to make next month's bill smaller? You can't bring together too much for an extra payment so the question is "how is just $10 going to help when I owe tens of thousands"?

The secret is taking the steps to making early and consistent extra payments. For example, on the home mortgage shown above, if you pay an additional $100 each month you will save over $82,000 in interest payments. Not only that, but you will also have your home paid off nine years and two months earlier. You knock nearly 10 years off your mortgage just by paying an extra $100 a month.

How does making extra payments work?

Every $100 extra you pay per month would have cost you about $270 in interest on the original amount you have borrowed for 30 years. Hence, when you made this extra payment you will have paid in excess, therefore, you will reduce your last mortgage payment by $270. The next month's extra payment will reduce your last mortgage payment by $268. Each month as you continually pay that extra $100, your final mortgage payment will be reduced until you won't need to make a final payment, then the second to last payment, then third creating a continuity of pay down of principle. As time wanes on, you will have shaved years and thousands of dollars in interest charges off your mortgage.

That's great, but maybe you are currently unable to spare $100 each month. How about considering, $50, $25 or even $10? An additional payment of $50 each month will save you five years and seven months and about $52,000 dollars. Twenty five dollars each month will cut your payment time by three years and three months saving you about $30,000. Just $10 a month will also reduce your payment time by one year and three months and save you over $13,500.

Don't dismay as every little bit helps. When you know that in some months you may be only able to add $10 to your payment; other months you may be able to pay an extra $200.

Taking in all aspects of loans and any other kind of debt you can apply this schelduling of payments to all interest bearing accounts, like credit card payments or vehicle repayment. Paying down as much of the principal (the amount owed) each month will help reduce the interest you are charged and the length of time it takes to pay off the debt.

So why don't the credit card companies charge you more of the principal each month? Credit card companies are a legal form of loan sharks.

How would you like to yield 18-23% on an investment? Wouldn't you want this investment to last as long as possible? Of course! So do the credit card companies. They are happy for you to pay off your balance, but even more excited for you to keep paying them that 20% interest.

Interest Tips and Tricks

- One trick your mortgage company may have played on you is to include a prepayment penalty in your mortgage. When you are paying off your mortgage early the mortgage holder may actually charge you for doing so. Another note is that they may only apply part of your payment to the principal and take the rest as a "service charge."

- When you intend to **make an additional payment**, it is important that you send a check separate from your monthly mortgage payment, including instructions that the amount is to be applied toward the principal of your loan. Without direction of how the payment is to be applied, they may just apply it towards next month's payment and still charge you the interest.

- In general you will not have this problem with credit card companies. **But watch out for late payments or going over your credit limit**. They may then use these "rule infractions" as cause to raise your rate to over 30%!

- If you are shopping to **refinance your mortgage**, ask for a mortgage that lets you **pay on a bi-weekly basis**. It may be easier for you to manage bi-weekly payments, as many people receive a bi-weekly paycheck. If you are paying every two weeks you will make an additional monthly payment each year (26 bi-weekly payments vs. 12 monthly payments). Additionally, because you are paying the principal down every two weeks rather than every month, your interest charges will be reduced.

You are more than able to absolutely take control of your interest charges and payments, rather than be controlled by them. It is important to make those extra monthly payments. The relief of the burden of the weight of debt; instead being debt-free, will far outweigh the temporary pleasures of any "great" product or a quiet evening that later becomes a debt.

The next thing about credit cards that need to be addressed is **QUIT using them**, unless of course you are paying them off each month, as you have ONLY purchased items that you had within your budget in first place. Reducing your debt is not achieved by delaying debt.

Keep your credit rating high. It's all about the numbers on the credit report. One of the things that you can do while you are paying down your debt and become debt free is to understand that closed credit accounts (department stores, Visa/MC/Discover cards) on your credit report that are in the revolving credit category will **dampen your credit rating**. So before you close those accounts consider taking the following approach, either cut up the credit card so you are not tempted to use it, or stick it in the freezer in a zip lock bag. AFTER you have paid off your debt, not just paid down, you can begin to add your use of the credit cards to the extent of what you are able to pay off each month, and will not get you behind on any current monthly obligations. You must take action and discipline yourself to make the right financial decisions that will not bury you and your household in financial debt and ruin.

5 - Determining Where You Are Financially

It starts with collecting all the information and writing it down. You can use a spreadsheet or a piece of paper and a calculator, whatever works for you.   Either way, you need to list every bill you are obligated to pay each month now. Next to it write down what your obligations will be after you are debt free! You will always have monthly bills for utilities and necessities.

Current Bills & Credit Obligations	Balance	Monthly Payment Amount	Date Due	Amount Paid
Tithe/Charity Contributions				
House payment/Rent				
Pay yourself/ Rainy day				
Vehicle payment				
Food/grocery				
Credit cards • Credit card • Credit card • Credit card • Credit card				
Utilities • Electric				

• Natural gas • Water/Sewer • Telephone/Cell • Cable/Dish • Internet				
Fuel for Vehicles				
Daycare Expense				
Co-pays/ Prescriptions				
Homeowners/ Renters Ins				
Vehicle Insurance				
Health Insurance				
Life Insurance				
Property Taxes				
Home Maintenance				
School activities				
Clothing				
Misc Allowance				

The above table is just an example of how to lay out your bills. Following you writing them down, it is still suggested that you use money managing software. However, even though you may use software to help guide you through your budget, it is always good to take time and review your written budget.

If you listen to the newscasts, you may find that you are not alone in your budget demise. Times are tough "all over", and it is going to take some discipline with your budget so you and your family can go through these apparent lean years ahead without losing everything you have worked for.

If you find that with the demands of your budget, there is too much month left at the end of your money, you have a few choices you are going to have to reckon with;

- You must **cut spending** immediately; you are not the USA government who can just print the money as needed.

- Once you have cut your spending and you find that there is still too much month and not enough money, additional hard decisions must be made.

- **Downsize**, if you know that you are unable to cut any further and all attempts to reduce your spending has been done. You might need to consider selling your home and purchase a home with lesser payment, or trade in your high priced vehicle for a more economical one.

- Clothing costs can become high, consider **buying your clothes** at **consignment shop, thrift store, and if the local discount department store** has not been the "place " to buy your clothing, perhaps it is a good time to consider shopping where indeed the prices are lower.

- **Do your own pool and lawn care**.

- **Get a part time job**; there are more part time jobs available than there are full time jobs.

- **Refinance your home**; if you have equity to a lower your payment at a fixed rate then pay off as many of your debts as possible.

6 - Greatest Secret

Have you ever had your Mother say to you, don't eat so fast, chew your food you might taste it?

The same theory applies to your budget. By keeping up with the Jones' and the Smith's, and who ever else you have found yourself in competition with in obtaining all of the "Good Life", did you ever consider that you were running yourself into the ground? Life has ups and downs, you only find out who you are when you are in the down part of life. How you face your needs and activities today when life has become a struggle, will reveal who you really are. If you have mistakenly sold your future for the here and now, your future is here now. You must step back and re-evaluate what your true destination is from this point forward.

The greatest secret is really no secret at all, it is the exercising of common sense. If you are out of practice of this type of exercising then let's review:

- You must have a plan and goals to follow

- You must be able to write your goals down

- You must be able to write you goals in the order you see them being accomplished

- You must have goals that you can see the results within one week and then built upon you will be able to see a goal accomplished in one month.

- You must look at your goals every day knowing that you are one day closer to reaching your goals

- You must not give up on your goals, no matter what the circumstances; your livelihood and survival through difficult times depend upon you sticking it through, as these times will end.

Any man or woman who has truly accomplished any feat in their life first had a goal. The most successful people have always known about making goals, which, writing down, the goals are just as important when undertaking a new task. Or remaking and reworking an old task that without the goal, the timeline has fallen apart. Once you get the goal out of your head and written down on paper you have made your physical self realize that your mind and mental self are now directing your physical path.

The saying "The mind is terrible thing to waste" really is true. It is important for you to realize that your mind can be one of the most resourceful tools in your weaponry. What you think you will become, how you think will create you. Don't waste time; get your mind on board, to bring your life into line with your goals and passions. As a person thinks so is he/she. It has been stated and restated by many diverse teachers and scholars that; "A person is what he/she thinks about all day long". So what are you thinking about?

7 - Your 30 Day Challenge

Before you start writing down what you are considering for your thirty day challenge, stop; evaluate what you really do want. What that means is do you know what your order of business is that you can work diligently toward and keep a focus on to see a result within thirty days. At the end of 30 days, renew the challenge!

With each thirty day challenge, the rules are the same:

1) Your challenge needs to be written down seven times on different reference cards, index cards works well. Places to put your 30 day cards:

   a) Place one card taped to your alarm clock to remind yourself of your challenge

   b) Taped to your bathroom mirror

   c) Fold one and place it around your debit card in your wallet

   d) On your dashboard or rearview mirror of your car

   e) Taped to your computer monitor at home and work

   f) Taped on or about your coffee pot.

2) You need to keep the card in your wallet

3) You need to look at it every day, read it and do at least one thing each day that will bring you closer to accomplishing your 30 day challenge.

4) If you for any reason break your 30 day challenge, you must restart from the beginning.

5) If you are married, you and your spouse should be on the same page of the thirty day challenge IF your challenge will effect them any way, working together to make your challenge come to fruition.

6) On the back side of your written down challenge write down these words and read them everyday when you read your thirty day challenge. "Knock and the door will open, seek and you shall find." And "You must become what you think about"

Once you establish which thirty day challenge that you are going to implement within your home, it is then you can get excited. Before you get too excited, use a little wisdom. As your thirty day challenge is a new thing, or something that you are reattempting to do, it is important for you to realize that, when a baby first learns to sit up, then crawl, then stand, walk, and then run, you too must not try to outsmart yourself and try to run before you really know how to sit up.

Here are some examples that will effectually reduce you monthly budget that can be used as a proving ground for you to eventually work finesse in your thirty day challenge.

1) For one month, do not eat out, either for lunch or dinner; instead make all of your meals at home. Take your lunch to work with you.

   a) Plan your meals ahead of time

   b) Prepare food ahead of time, storing it in lunch containers either directly after dinner for the lunch tomorrow or doing a few lunches up ahead of time and put in the freezer for lunches or for a quick meal at dinner when you are too tired to cook.

   c) Use coupons to save in your grocery shopping at www.inmyalley.com or found in your Sunday newspaper.

2) For one month, watch where you spend money, write down every penny you spend in a little notebook for one month to track ALL of your spending. Once you implement this strategy, success is forthcoming!

3) Turn off lights and shut down anything that requires electricity, when you leave that room, even if you are going back to be right back in that room, with

exceptions of clocks, refrigerator, freezer and stove. There may be other major appliances that you will not turn off, however realize that the computer that is left on, the television although off is pulling a trickle amount of electricity that, like a leaky faucet, adds to your monthly bills.

4) Contact your service providers and drop extra services and/or negotiate lower rates.

5) Remove the credit cards from your wallet. Eliminate the temptation!

Just doing one of these examples above will save you money. Before you discount these suggestions, thinking what good will that little bit of savings and awareness do for my budget; listen are you doing anything now?

The previous are just examples of 30 day challenges; you will have your own priorities of what is important to you. If you have a pressing matter that needs to be addressed, whether it is foreclosure or vehicle repossession, do address those immediately, and know that if you are faithful with a little, then you will be faithful with much. You must make a stand before you walk, but you need to know what you're standing on.

Stopping the leakage

Since you have been tracking where you spend your money, you now know where you have to stop your spending. In fact you will have on pen and paper, where you have been spending to know where your leakage is coming from.

Perhaps the biggest mistake of budgeting is not budgeting in your miscellaneous allowance. That sum of money you have given unto yourself to spend however you want. If you over criticize your budget it will be your downfall, just like the over zealous diet that restricts 100% from your "favorite" food of choice. A small allowance, like having a pizza or the chocolate bar or one latte upon occasion, will not upset your diet, but instead keeping within your boundaries will not make your diet intolerable. Your new self discipline will enable you to stick with your budget. As in this case of giving yourself an allowance to spend any way that you can afford within that allowance, you will not upset your budget.

- Identify your wasteful spending
- Give yourself an allowance
- Understand if you go over your allowance you must give up something in your budget
- You do not have a money tree in the backyard

Wages and how to work within them

Wages of salaried employees or management persons do not change, simplifying the budget planning process. You know exactly what you are going to receive every pay check. Most, but not all salaried employees have an optional 401k that they can contribute to each pay period. Consider participating with the 401k if you have not already – it is a good place to cover your savings needs for your future. If your employer contributes as well when you participate in the 401k, it would be ridiculous not to take advantage of the free money that they offer when you participate.

If your employer offers any opportunity to gain "free assets" use them, from 401k to stock in the company. Of course as you get your budget under control and balanced you will want to expand your personal savings beyond what your employer offers. Just keep in mind, that whatever program that your employer offers that is pre-tax, or that they themselves contribute to with you, is like giving yourself a raise.

Hourly employees have to be on the job to get their hourly wage. Most hourly employees are not afforded the opportunity to participate in a 401k, however if you do have that opportunity, check into the offer that your employers may offer, especially if they are contributing to your 401k. The pre-tax disbursement would be an asset as well, as it lowers your taxed income amount allowing for you to have money saved that is working for you fully.

(Note: when you withdraw from a 401k that money is taxable immediately, unless placed into another 401k.)

Commissioned employees are typically classified as sales; however there are still some other jobs that fall under the commission umbrella. For instance some hairstylists are commissioned employees, as are massage therapists and other service oriented employees. Most commissioned employees have little to no benefits available to them. Most employers of commissioned employees think that the employee, if they are good to great at their job, should be able to afford their own benefit package. However, there are good months and bad months within any commissioned based employment; a great employer will offer some great benefits for their commissioned employees. If your employer does offer any benefits, take advantage of them.

Tipped employees may find themselves in the commissioned employee status. Similar to a food server, you are dependent upon the customer flow into your station. Your "check" from your employer is typically only a few dollars per hour. If you have never been a server then you may not know that servers in general get paid around $3.13 per hour, as employers of servers do not deem that they need spend any more on employee costs as the server is being paid by the customer for their service. However, even a great server cannot keep the customers coming back without good food and a pleasing atmosphere.

A tipped employee needs to be the most diligent in their budgeting as it can become easy to spend the money in your pocket as you are working tomorrow and you can make up your house or rent payment... not true in this unstable economy. The tipped based employees are either on one end of the spectrum or the other. They either are great money managers or so poor that they are broke from day to day. The 30 day challenge for the tipped employee is a great tool on how to get started in balanced money management.

8 - Balancing Your Checkbook

Perhaps one of the most overlooked aspects of any budget is the balancing your check book. The register is not a waste of printed paper. The bank cordially offers you an avenue to keep your finances in order. There have been those who for lack of understanding and knowledge thought that as long as they had checks they had money.

When the ATM machines came on line to be used, many found that the ease of access to their money quickly led to overdrafts on their accounts. At $30 plus per overdraft it became a nightmare.

Online banking is a tool, not your bank register. While utilizing the bank online tools is a great way to pay bills and save money on postage and envelopes, it is not your accountant.

Before setting up a checking account you need to know what your needs are and what you expect of your bank.

Here are some things to consider:

- Free checking availability - Many banks offer free checking with a low account opening balance while others require a minimum balance of $500 or more.

- Do you want to have an automated savings account with your checking? Some banking institutions offer a connected savings account that takes $1 dollar from your checking account every time you use your debit card and adds it to your savings account. This is a great way to save a little at a time yet adds up to a sizeable savings. However since it will be deducted from your checking account, don't forget to deduct the transfer in your bank register.

- Free access to ATM machines with your debit card. Not all ATM's allow you to access your account for cash for free. If you find that you must draw from your account from an ATM that charges, don't forget to deduct that from your checkbook register.

- Some free checking is only available if you have at least one auto deposit occurrence each month. If you change your job, you will need to sign up for direct deposit. If the time lapse is longer than one month you may face a monthly charge for your checking account. Also if you have auto pay for some bills and you have been issued a hard check rather than auto deposit, until the direct deposit is established you may incur overdrafts if you haven't accounted for auto pay withdrawals. Make plans for how you pay your bills during the time your direct deposit requests are processed.

- Do you write a lot of checks? The number of checks you use may determine whether free checking is available.
- Opening and sustaining a savings account to prevent overdraft. This is where you open a savings account connected to your checking, (not the same as above), that you designate for protection against over drafting your account and having an auto-pay or other service rejected because of lack of funds. Note: Some savings overdraft protection will still create an overdraft fee, some will not. You will need to inquire into the overdraft policy when you set up your account. Additionally, some institutions will charge you interest on overdrafts, again you need to inquire of your institutions' policy.

Checking Tips:
1. Check off cleared items in your register. As your debits on your account are posted within online banking, or when you receive your bank statement you need to reconcile your account. Verify all transactions against your bank register. Check them off in your register, validate each item.
2. Reconcile your check book. If you don't carry your physical checkbook with you throughout the day to immediately input what you have spent with your debit card, then ALWAYS get the receipt and

keep it in your wallet to be entered in your checkbook when you get home. With online checking you can check your account for activity and compare that document to your current check register. This is so #1, your entry is the same as you were billed and, #2 you make sure that a transaction hasn't been missed.

3. A detailed account of your transactions will assist you if you feel like you have a complaint with your bank and what they say is your balance and what you have as your balance. Everyone makes mistakes, from you to the teller and whoever else may be involved with your bank transactions, or even in the case of duplicate processing of one transaction.

4. Using your debit card with a VISA/MasterCard logo is a convenience for you and the merchant. However you can overdraw your account with your VISA/MasterCard debit card rather easily if you have not kept an account of your spending in your register. At $30 plus charge for every overdraft incurred, you can easily overturn your budget. You will have to catch up your overdrafts before you can continue to pay your bills.

5. Many retail stores and institutions use check clearing for automatic transfers. For instance if you write a check at Wal-Mart, as soon as you hand the check to the cashier they will run your

check through a NIC scanner and the amount is immediately drafted from your account.

6. Debit cards usage can either have a delay of 24 hours or again, be an immediate withdrawal. Don't count on it being the 24 hour delay, have the funds in your account or suffer an overdraft fee.

7. Your bank statements are just as important as your register. You will need them to get loans, especially if you are seeking a loan from an institution other than your bank. Also if you have paid off a creditor, and at sometime in the future you find that there records are lost, mishandled, an entry mistake, or any other type of missed accounting records, YOU, not the creditor must prove that you have indeed paid that debt. So whether you are getting statements in snail mail or email, keep good records of your finances.

8. IF you have abused your privileges with your banking institute be aware that they may indeed hold any check deposit you make up to 10 days, whether it be a personal check or a payroll check.

9. If you find that you have revoked privileges with your institution, nearly 100% of the time you will not be able to open another account with another institution until you have reconciled monies with your first bank.

A typical check register will have 8 columns in each row;

- First column date of transaction
- Second column debit or check number
- Third column vendor/retail/personal name to whom the funds went out to.
- Fourth column amount of transaction
- Fifth column to check off when it has cleared the bank
- Sixth column to indicate a fee (i.e., ATM fee)
- Seventh column is where deposit amounts are entered
- Eighth column for running balance in your account

Number	Date	Description	Payment Amt.	✔	Fee	Deposit Amount	Balance
101	7/10	Target	$27.52	✔			$247.76
-	7/12	Deposit		✔		$500.00	$747.76
Debit	7/16	Mobil	$31.32	✔			$716.44

Check cashing without having a bank account is difficult and costly; difficult in the terms of finding an institution to cash a check, especially if it is not drawn on their institution. Check cashing places charge $25 dollars or more to cash your payroll check. If you are paid weekly the cost will be $100. That is a lot to pay to have your check cashed. Some grocery stores will cash your payroll check at customer service counters again with a minimum to maximum fee based upon the amount of your check.

Beware!

Check fraud and Visa Debit fraud is increasing. Protect your accounts. Don't leave your checkbook lying around, as someone could remove a check from it, from the back of your checkbook, and then write a check, before you know the check is missing. Another issue is the debit card, when it is being used as credit/debit say at gas station. Be sure to inspect the card slot for a foreign object in the slot. If you are unsure, DON'T USE IT! Card data theft devices are being used when you slide your card into the slot, capturing your pin, zip and account number. Card fraud is a quick process; perpetrators are capturing your data, stealing it and using it within minutes of your transaction, draining your account completely within a few short minutes to an hour's time.

Kiting checks is not just a big NO-NO, it is fraud and punishable in a court of law. An example of check kiting fraud is if you write a check that does not have the funds available in that checking account you have wrote from, but you are going to cover it with another check from a different bank account to cover the amount, that account also does not have the funds to cover the written check. So plain and simple you write a check for $25.00 from bank account A, which does not have enough to cover the expense, then you write a check for bank account B say $50.00 to be deposited in account A to cover the expense, yet account B does not have enough to cover the $50.00, so the next day you write another check from account A of $75.00 to account B. This is kiting - trying to cover what you are purchasing when you have no money. So by the time that payday does come you have kited all of your income away. Many have also done this with credit cards only to find themselves deeply in debt.

9 - Savings - Start Today and Watch It Grow

You may have heard an old but simply true statement, "That what a man sows he shall reap". If you haven't any savings it just means that more than likely you haven't saved. The only exception is that you have had such a rainy day that you have used up your savings. But for the most part, no matter what the economy you should be saving for your future. If you have no plan and performance of savings, then you are planning to fail.

Ways to save

- Save ten percent of every check

- Pick up every penny you see lying on the ground

- Put your coin aside

- Take 20% of your savings that you have and invest in a Roth fund at the bank

- When you have maximized your Roth deposit allowance, follow it up with a Money CD for a couple of maturities

- Talk with your bank on what they offer to invest you money

- Buy whole life insurance as it can be an excellent way to grow your money talk. Don't freak out when you find that the policy premiums are indeed greater. The idea is this; the whole life insurance policy will grow into maturity and is available to be cashed out if need be. Just like a home mortgage is different than renting, you can usually count on your home to grow in value and you can sell later, the whole life insurance plan works the same way.

No matter what your choice of savings may be, just do it and watch it grow. You will see that what you sow (money in savings) you shall reap (interest on savings account or investments that grow). If you plant a garden you don't expect to eat dirt! If you don't plant anything then you will eat dirt!

10 - Considering Bankruptcy

If you find that you are considering bankruptcy, we have provided general bankruptcy information that you need to make an informed decision. After reading the following FAQ information, you will have a good understanding of what the law before you meet with a Lawyer, Barrister or Attorney.

Before you begin to think that you are a "bad finance manager", understand that you may have been the absolute best money manager that the neighborhood has ever seen, but you have encountered a string of bad luck. Here is a list of the most common reasons for those finding themselves on the brink or filing for bankruptcy:

1. Medical bills

2. Loss of employment

3. Wage garnishments

4. Cannot meet bill obligations after a divorce

5. Large credit card debt

6. To buy time to keep your home/car from being repossessed, to allow you to catch up on the payments

7. Divorce

A Few Reasons Not to File Bankruptcy

Before you pull your hair out and begin to run yourself down to ground level, here are some of the reasons why you should not file bankruptcy, along with some possible alternatives.

YOUR DEBT IS NOT A LARGE DEBT

- If you only have limited debt or if creditors claim you owe debts that you did not incur and you feel overwhelmed, then taking the initiative to combat a debt that you do not believe you owe might enable you to utilize other options other than filing for bankruptcy. For example, with enough of a paper trail proving your case of wrongful credit claims, you could bring or defend a court case to challenge the existence of the debt.

WHEN ALL OF YOUR PROPERTY IS "EXEMPT"

- If all of your property is exempt (such as the home you are living in and a vehicle) it may be desirable, but not always necessary, to file for bankruptcy to protect it. If the credit card hounds are barking at your door, there are some reputable credit counselors that can (for a customary fee of $50.00

per credit issue) help you to resolve your dilemma.

YOU MIGHT LOSE YOUR "NON-EXEMPT PROPERTY"

- In a Chapter 7 bankruptcy, if you have substantial assets over and above the exemption limits (some examples include; second or investment homes, RVs, additional vehicles, boats, recently acquired assets or investments within the last 18 months) they will be deemed desirable to be turned over to a bankruptcy trustee and sold to pay off your creditors.

THE AFFECT A BANKRUPTCY WILL HAVE ON YOUR CREDIT

- Bankruptcy will have an affect on your credit profile. A bankruptcy filing can stay on your credit report for ten (10) years. Even if you file bankruptcy, and then locate another alternative, and you decided to dismiss your bankruptcy petition, *the filing* can be, and probably will be, on your credit report for up to ten years. It is important to note, the effect of such a report on your future credit is not always predictable and is independently scrutinized by any new creditors. It is also important to realize that, if you have substantial debts for which you are now in default, and do not foresee being able to clear them up, you already have a poor credit history. A bankruptcy will wipe the credit slate clean, enabling you to a fresh start. It may be viewed by some, not all, creditors as an improvement, and issue you a credit line.

BANKRUPTCY MAY NOT OFFER HELP IN YOUR SITUATION, OR BANKRUPTCY INDEED MAY HURT YOU

- In some cases, a bankruptcy will speed up the loss of property rather than prevent it. Major debts, including but not limited to, tax liens, or for that matter most liens, may be in the classification of those that are not dischargeable.

You expect to continue to go deeper into debt.

- In this situation, it might be best to delay and waiting, before filing for bankruptcy until you have accrued all of the debt that you foresee, as in medical treament. Medical bills that are piling up while you are either in process or in recovery with the possibility of accruing more, would be a reason to delay a bankruptcy until all the medical bills have been processed and you are in good health.

- While you may have an obese budget to date, there are many steps to overcoming your debt to income ratio. Those steps have been aforementioned, however, if you can see no way out of your demise, whether self-inflicted or a victim of extreme finance stretching not created with intent to defraud credit merchants, then the following chapter can help you to determine the type of bankruptcy that may be appropriate for your situation.

Credit Counseling

The following Credit Counseling information was extracted from the Federal Trade Commission website at:
http://www.ftc.gov/bcp/edu/pubs/consumer/credit/cre41.shtm

With limited exceptions, people who plan to file for bankruptcy protection must get credit counseling from a government-approved organization within 180 days before they file. They also must complete a debtor education course to have their debts discharged. As a rule, pre-bankruptcy credit counseling and pre-discharge debtor education may not be provided at the same time. Credit counseling must take place before you file for bankruptcy; debtor education must take place after you file.

In general, you must file a certificate of credit counseling completion when you file for bankruptcy and evidence of completion of debtor education after you file for bankruptcy – but before your debts are discharged. Only credit counseling organizations and debtor education course providers that have been approved by the U.S. Trustee Program may issue these certificates. To protect against fraud, the certificates are produced through a central automated system and are numbered.

A pre-bankruptcy counseling session with an approved credit counseling organization should include an evaluation of your personal financial situation, a discussion of alternatives to bankruptcy, and a personal budget plan. A typical counseling session should last about 60 to 90 minutes, and can take place in person, on the phone, or online. The counseling organization is required to provide the counseling free of charge for those consumers who cannot afford to pay. If you cannot afford to pay a fee for credit counseling, you should request a fee waiver from the counseling organization before the session begins. Otherwise, you may be charged a fee for the counseling, which will generally be about $50, depending on where you live, the types of services you receive, and other factors. The counseling organization is required to discuss any fees with you before starting the counseling session.

Once you have completed the required counseling, you must get a certificate as proof. Check the U.S. Trustee's website to be sure that you receive the certificate from a counseling organization that is approved in the judicial district where you are filing bankruptcy. Credit counseling organizations may not charge an extra fee for the certificate.

Important Questions to Ask When Choosing a Credit Counselor

It's wise to do some research when choosing a credit counseling organization. If you are in search of credit counseling to fulfill the bankruptcy law requirements, make sure you receive services only from approved providers for your judicial district. Check the list at www.usdoj.gov/ust/eo/bapcpa/ccde/cc_approved.htm or at the bankruptcy clerk's office for the district where you will file. Once you have the list of approved organizations in your judicial district, call several to gather information before you make your choice. Some key questions to ask are:

- What services do you offer?

- Will you help me develop a plan for avoiding problems in the future?

- What are your fees?

- What if I can't afford to pay your fees?

- What qualifications do your counselors have? Are they accredited or certified by an outside organization? What training do they receive?

- What do you do to keep information about me (including my address, phone number, and financial information) confidential and secure?

- How are your employees paid? Are they paid more if I sign up for certain services, if I pay a fee, or if I make a contribution to your organization?

11 - Chapter 7 Bankruptcy

Chapter 7 bankruptcies, or are sometimes referred as a straight bankruptcy, it is a liquidation proceeding. The debtor turns over all non-exempt property to the bankruptcy trustee, who then converts the assets into cash for distribution to the creditors. The debtor receives a discharge of all dischargeable debts usually within four months. In the vast majority of cases, the debtor has no assets of value that he would lose. So, Chapter 7 will give that person a relatively quick "fresh start".

One of the main purposes of Bankruptcy Law is to give a person, who is hopelessly burdened with debt, a fresh start by wiping out his or her debts.

Most Common Reasons for a Chapter 7 Bankruptcy
- Unemployment
- Large medical expenses
- Seriously overextended credit
- Marital problems
- Other large unexpected expenses

A Harvard Study recently reported its findings (2005) that more than half of US bankruptcies were caused by medical Bills (MSNBC). The study was published online in

February of 2005 by <u>Health Affairs</u>. *The Harvard study concluded that illness and medical bills caused half (50.4 percent) of the 1,458,000 personal bankruptcies in 2001. The study estimates that medical bankruptcies affect about 2 million Americans annually* — counting debtors and their dependents, including about 700,000 children. Today's numbers of bankruptcies has climbed due to torrential fallout of the economy issues. The number fluctuation on month by month basis of bankruptcy filings is rising as the economy spirals downward.

Common Questions and Answers Regarding Bankruptcy

Will it be difficult to file Chapter 7 under the new Bankruptcy Laws?

There has been much doom and gloom written about the bankruptcy means test, the new laws have changed the previous avenues of filing, indeed it is much more difficult it's to file Chapter 7. It's true that there are more hoops to jump through under the new laws and it's true that the bankruptcy means test will result in some people having to file Chapter 13 instead of Chapter 7. **However, for the vast majority of fllers, Chapter 7 is still available with very little extra effort! Make the effort pay off with due diligence on your part.**

Will my creditors stop harassing me?

Yes, they will! By law, all actions, by creditors to pursue payment, against a debtor must cease once the documents are filed. Creditors cannot initiate or continue any lawsuits, wage garnishees, or even telephone calls demanding payments. Secured creditors, (who hold collateral on an item) such as banks holding, for example, a lien on a car, will get the stay, (cease and desist) lifted if you cannot make payments.

Will my spouse/or other family be affected by my filing?

Your wife or husband, or anyone else besides yourself, will not be affected by your bankruptcy if **they are not responsible** (they did not sign an agreement or contract) for any of your debt. If they have supplemental credit cards, or properties purchased, they are probably responsible for that debt. However, in community property states, either spouse can contract for a debt without the other spouse's signature on anything, and still obligate the marital community. There are a few exceptions to that rule, such as the purchase or sale of real estate; those few exceptions do require both spouses' signatures on contracts. But the day to day debts, such as credit cards, do NOT require both spouses to have signed.

Community property states are listed for your convenience: Arizona, California, Idaho, Louisiana, Nevada, New Mexico, Texas, Washington and Wisconsin.

Your lawyer will be able to guide you in this process.

Who will know?

Bankruptcy filings are public records. However, under normal circumstances, no one will know you went bankrupt. Some employers have different criteria to meet and may deem a bankruptcy poorly. The current 3 Credit Bureaus will record your bankruptcy and it will remain on your credit record for 10 years.

What will I keep?

In a bankruptcy, assets in excess of your allowed personal exemption, or non exempt assets such as, real estate, automobiles and boats will be liquidated and converted to pay debts, by the trustee.

I was bankrupt before – when can I file again?

A person can file Chapter 7 again if it has been more than 8 years since he or she filed the previous Chapter 7 bankruptcy. Also refer to: Filing on **Chapter 13.**

Can I keep any credit cards?

Whether a debtor keeps credit cards after filing bankruptcy is up to the credit card company. If you are discharging a credit card they will cancel the card unless you reaffirm the debt. Even if you have a zero balance the credit card company might cancel the card. The credit card companies that you have accounts with, will independently determine if they will continue to service your financial needs.

When will I be discharged from Bankruptcy?

One of the major purposes of bankruptcy legislation is to afford the opportunity to a person hopelessly burdened with debt to erase his or her debt and thereby enabling a person to get a fresh financial start. A bankrupt's debt is erased when he or she is discharged. Upon receiving your discharge keep that paper in a safe place for the entire 10 years.

The debtor is discharged 3 - 5 months after bankruptcy is filed. At that time all debts (with some exceptions) are written off. Be sure to know what was not discharged.

Will I ever get credit again?

Yes! A number of banks now offer "secured" credit cards where a debtor puts up a certain amount of money (as little as $200) in an account at the bank to guarantee payment. Your personal bank may set you up a secured card account. Usually the credit limit is equal to the security given and is increased over time as the debtor proves his or her ability to pay the debt. Currently it is two years after a bankruptcy discharge, debtors are eligible for mortgage loans on terms as good as those of others, with the same financial profile, as those whom have not filed bankruptcy. Again, note that you must establish a good payment history after bankruptcy. **The size of your down payment and the stability of your income** will be much more important than the fact you filed bankruptcy in the past.The fact you filed bankruptcy stays on your credit report for 10 years, the facts after bankruptcy is just as important to a lender. It becomes less significant as time passes on the further in the past the bankruptcy is and your up keep on your current credit is maintained. The truth is, as odd as it may seem that you are probably a better credit risk after bankruptcy than before.

Can my boss fire me for filing Bankruptcy?

No. U.S.C. Sec. 525 prohibits any employer from discriminating against you because you filed bankruptcy.

How much am I allowed to keep?

You are allowed to keep certain assets; the court trustee will make that determination, not you, depending on the state in which you reside.

What debts are erased by a Bankruptcy?

Most unsecured debt is erased in a bankruptcy except for:

a) Child support and alimony

b) Debts for personal injury or death caused by your drunk driving

c) Student Loans

d) Income tax debt

Note on Private Student Loans: *On June 7, 2007, US Senator Dick Durbin introduced a Bill to make private student loans dischargeable in bankruptcy, as they were before 2005. The 2005 changes to the U.S. Bankruptcy Code made the treatment of private student loans equivalent to the treatment of government-guaranteed student loans, which were not dischargeable. This bill would reverse the 2005 amendment, so that private student loans again would be fully dischargeable in bankruptcy.*

What does it cost?

It costs about $300-$500 to file a Chapter 7 bankruptcy. A bankruptcy lawyer's fees vary but should be in the range of $1,000 to $2,000. Many bankruptcy lawyers will offer you a free initial consultation. You can keep the fees down by being well organized and well prepared with all of the creditors owed and outstanding bills in hand. You may also be able to keep the fees down by not requiring the lawyer to attend the meeting of creditors with you. Check with your lawyer, to determine if you are capable to handle yourself in the proceeding. In some states, such as Massachusetts, attorneys must attend the Section 341 meeting with the debtors otherwise attorneys are deemed to have NOT represented the debtors at the 341 Meeting.

Will Chapter 7 wipe out my federal income tax debt?

You can discharge (wipe out) debts for federal income taxes in Chapter 7 bankruptcy only if all of these five conditions are true:

1) The taxes are income taxes. Taxes other than income, such as payroll taxes, Trust Fund Recovery Penalty or fraud penalties, can never be eliminated in bankruptcy.

2) You did not commit fraud or willful evasion. You did not file a fraudulent tax return or otherwise willfully attempt to evade paying taxes, such as using a false Social Security number on your tax return.

3) You pass the three-year rule. The tax return was originally due **at least** three years before you file for bankruptcy. Consult with your attorney on this as they will have a better insight on the timeline for you, additionally laws are changing constantly so be aware of your rights.

4) You pass the two-year rule. You actually filed the tax return at least two years before filing the bankruptcy -- having the IRS file a substitute return for you will not count unless you agreed to and signed the substitute return.

5) You pass the 240-day rule. The income tax debt was assessed by the IRS at least 240 days before you file your bankruptcy petition, or has not yet been assessed.

If any of the following situations apply to you, you will have to add time to the three-year, two-year or 240-day rules for your debts to qualify for discharge in bankruptcy:

1) If you submitted an Offer in Compromise, the 240-day rule is delayed by the period of time from when the Offer is made until the IRS rejects it or you withdraw it, plus 30 days.

2) If you obtained a Taxpayer Assistance Order from an IRS Problems Resolution Officer preventing the IRS from collecting, the bankruptcy court may require that you add the time collection was suspended to the three-year, two-year and 240-day requirements.

3) If you filed a previous bankruptcy case, all three time periods stopped running while you were in the prior

bankruptcy case. You must add the length of your case plus six months to all three.

Caution! A Chapter 7 bankruptcy will wipe out only your personal obligation to pay the debt. Any lien recorded, be sure to address any lien as that can be a black mark for rebuilding your credit, before you file for bankruptcy will remain intact on your credit file.

After your bankruptcy, the IRS can and will seize any property you owned at the time the bankruptcy was file. However, this doesn't mean that after your bankruptcy case is over, the IRS will come and grab your property. Post-Bankruptcy, the IRS tends to seize only viable and tangible assets, real estate and retirement accounts or pensions. And even then, IRS seizures, generally, take place only when there is a real asset to acquire to pay your debt. Consult with your lawyer to determine what assets the IRS may be inquiring about after your file.

12 - Chapter 13 Bankruptcy

Chapter 13 bankruptcy is also known as the reorganization bankruptcy. It is filed by individuals, or, sole owned businesses, who want to pay off their debts over a period of three to five years. This type of bankruptcy appeals these types of individuals who have non-exempt property that they want to keep. It is also the only an option for businesses or individuals who have predictable income and whose income is sufficient to pay their reasonable expenses with some amount left over to pay off their debts.

There are many reasons why people choose Chapter 13 bankruptcy instead of Chapter 7 bankruptcy. Generally, you are probably a good candidate for Chapter 13 bankruptcy if you are in any of the following situations:

1) You have a sincere desire to repay your debts, but you need the protection of the bankruptcy court to do so. You may think filing Chapter 13 bankruptcy is simply the "Right Thing to Do", paying your incurred debts, rather than file Chapter 7.

2) You are behind on your mortgage or car loan, and want to make up the missed payments over time and reinstate the original agreement. You cannot do this

in Chapter 7 bankruptcy. You can make up missed payments only in Chapter 13 bankruptcy.

3) You need help repaying your debts now, but need to leave open the option of filing for Chapter 7 bankruptcy in the future. This would be the case if for some reason you can't stop incurring new debt, such as illness or a failing economy that may turn around.

4) You are a family farmer who wants to pay off your debts, but you do not qualify for a Chapter 12 family farming bankruptcy because you have a large debt unrelated to farming.

5) You have valuable nonexempt property. When you file for Chapter 7 bankruptcy, you get to keep certain property, called exempt. If you have a lot of nonexempt property (which you'd have to give up if you file a Chapter 7 bankruptcy), Chapter 13 bankruptcy may be the better option. You filed a Chapter 7 bankruptcy within the previous eight years. You cannot file for Chapter 7 again until the eight years are up.

Chapter 13 can be filed if:

1) The debtor received a discharge under Chapter 7, 11 or 12 more than four years ago; or

2) The debtor received a discharge under Chapter 13 more than two years ago.

3) You have a co-debtor, partnership, co-signer, on a personal debt. If you file for Chapter 7 bankruptcy, your creditor will go after the co-signer for payment. If you file for Chapter 13 bankruptcy, the creditor will leave your co-signer alone, as *long as you keep up with your bankruptcy plan payments.*

4) You have a tax debt. If a large part of your debt consists of federal taxes, what happens to your tax debts may determine which type of bankruptcy is best for you, a tax lawyer working with your bankruptcy lawyer, or a bankruptcy lawyer who specializes in the tax world would be an excellent choice when searching for a counselor.

Chapter 13 cannot be filed unless:

1) When a motor vehicle was purchased within 910 days (2 1/2 years) of the filing and a secured creditor has a lien on it, the creditor retains the lien until payment of the entire debt has been made.

2) The following incurred debt is NOT discharged:

   a) debt for trust fund taxes;

b) taxes for which returns were never filed or filed late (within two years of the petition date);

c) taxes for which the debtor made a fraudulent return or evaded taxes;

d) domestic support payments;

e) student loans; government or private

f) drunk driving injuries;

g) criminal restitution;

h) Civil restitutions or damages awarded for willful or malicious personal actions causing personal injury or death.

3) All tax returns for the four years prior to filing Chapter 13 must be filed.

4) Debtors must provide to the trustee, at least seven days prior to the 341 meeting, a copy of a tax return or transcript of a tax return, for the period for which the return was most recently due.

When can Chapter 13 be used?

Individuals may file chapter 13 bankruptcy petitions if they:

1) Reside, have a domicile, a place of business, or property in the United States, or a municipality;

2) Have a source of regular income; and on the date the petition is filed owe less than $290,525 in unsecured debts and less than $871,550 in secured debts. Note: The amounts given here are 2001 amounts. They are regularly adjusted to keep up with the cost of living.

Corporations and partnerships may not file a chapter 13 bankruptcy petition. If you filed a prior bankruptcy petition and the prior proceeding was dismissed within the last 180 days, you may not be able to file a second petition and should check 11 U.S.C. sec. 109(g).

Debt that might survive bankruptcy

The following debts are not erased in both Chapter 7 and Chapter 13. If you file for Chapter 7, these will remain when your case is over. If you file for Chapter 13, these debts will have to be paid in full during your plan. If they are not, the balance will remain at the end of your case:

1) Debts you forgot to list in your bankruptcy papers were filed, unless the creditor learns of your bankruptcy case;

2) Child support and alimony;

3) Debts for personal injury or death caused by your intoxicated driving;

4) Student loans from government organizations, unless it would be an undue hardship for you to repay;

5) Fines and penalties imposed for violating the law, such as traffic tickets and criminal restitution, and

6) Recent income tax debts and all other tax debts.

7) **This is a complicated area of the bankruptcy law and an attorney should be consulted.** You can discharge (wipe out) debts for federal income taxes in Chapter 7 bankruptcy only if all of these five conditions are met:

a) The IRS has not recorded a tax lien against your property. (If all other conditions are met, the taxes may be discharged, but even after your bankruptcy, the lien remains against all property you own, effectively giving the IRS a way to collect.)

b) You didn't file a fraudulent return.

c) You didn't try to evade paying taxes.

d) The liability is for a tax return (not a Substitute or Return) actually filed at least two years before you file for bankruptcy. The tax return was due at least three years ago.

e) The taxes were assessed (you received a notice of assessment of federal taxes from the IRS) at least 240 days (eight months) before you file for bankruptcy. (11 U.S.C. §§ 523(a) (1) and (7).)

8) In addition, the following debts may be declared **non-dischargeable** by a bankruptcy judge in Chapter 7 if the creditor challenges your request to discharge them. These debts may be discharged in Chapter 13. You can include them in your plan, and at the end of your case, the balance is wiped out:

a) Debts you incurred on the basis of fraud, such as lying on a credit application;

b) Credit purchases of $1,225 or more for luxury goods or services made within 60 days of filing;

c) Loans or cash advances of $1,225 or more taken within 60 days of filing;

d) Credit purchases of $500 or more for luxury goods or services made within 90 days of filing;

e) Loans or cash advances of $750 or more taken within 70 days of filing;

f) Debts from willful or malicious injury to another person or another person's property;

g) Debts from embezzlement, larceny or breach of trust, and

h) Debts you owe under a divorce decree or settlement unless after bankruptcy you would still not be able to afford to pay them or the benefit you'd receive by the discharge outweighs any detriment to your ex-spouse (who would have to be responsible to pay them if you discharge them in bankruptcy).

13 - Bringing It All Together

- Define to **yourself and your spouse** where you are at NOW in your budget

- Write out your budget needs

- Know your limits

- Make yourself a 30 day challenge

- Secure your future, plan your success

Set your goals

Sit down, breathe and relax, if you skip any of these steps you will not be ready to deal with your future. Yes YOUR future. The average persons within our society do not write down their goals. As a matter of fact, most people will tell you they have goals, the trick is to write them down and put them in front of you to be seen every day. When you are seeing yourself working through your goal, step by step, towards the completion of the goal, you will reach your goal. You must SEE yourself having and attaining your goal.

Do not be discouraged if you are detained from reaching your goal, delay is not denial! If you find yourself stopping just short of reaching your goal because of distractions... that will become your downfall. If you create in your mind what your personal world will look like everyday, it is within your reach and getting closer everyday. You must make it real to you.

There are many examples of great inventors of our history that have accomplished and produced many conveniences that we still enjoy today. The inventions of the light bulb, car, rubber tires, Tupperware, microwave ovens, windmills that either produce energy or pump water, the list goes on and on. Each of these awesome tools and conveniences first came from someone's mind. First conceived in the mind, seen from the mind, so believable that the heart and soul believed it, that the hands and feet of the inventors never stopped until they achieved what the mind conceived.

If you conceive an idea or direction and can see the end before the beginning, then believe that you will make happen what you have conceived, and then your belief will lead you to achieve your goal. If you think that it is impossible, it is. If you think it is possible, it is. No matter how you slice It, you are right either way.

So set your goals. See yourself completing your goals, work toward your goals and you will experience your goals. Your mind is so powerful that you can create what ever it conceives when you put action to the vision.

Setting yourself up for success - Making your budget work for you not against you

Planning your budget for the future is perhaps the biggest challenge that a person can come up against. Yes against. You must plan for your financial responsibilities. As with any diet, the fat did not show up over night, neither did your bills to creditors. So you must follow a simple formula that you are able to work with and follow through.

Take into consideration that, first things first, become debt free. WOW! What an awesome concept, to be debt free! Imagine that you have a large bucket, and you have next to the bucket some large stones, and then some smaller stones, then pebbles and finally gravel. Like your budget, you must begin to break it down to different categories. Within the categories of your budget you must first determine the dominant priorities of your budget.

When asked how I have been able to make my personal budget demands I primarily base its success on the one fact, I tithe at least 10% of my income to my church. Within my budget bucket, the first thing I put in and complete is my tithe. Secondly my house/apt payment, vehicle payment, then utilities, food, insurance, credit card and loans. Then as the stones turn to pebbles in my budget bucket, I put in the cell phone bill, internet, and finally miscellaneous items like clothing aside.

As most people can attest to, paying down payments to get them paid off, whether it is your credit cards, personal loans, vehicle loans, or mortgage is a challenge but you can do exactly this, pay your payments in such a manner that you have them paid off in a short span of time, a few months or a hand full of years in comparison to a lifetime.

Take a piece of paper, or use budget software of your choice, enter in your obligations, classifying by the rate of interest or penalties that may have been assessed to an existing credit card or, by highest rate of interest, to the lowest rate. In the beginning of your quest to bring your budget under control, you must make a decision, a commitment, to yourself and with your spouse that, you are going to follow through and be faithful to making an extra payment.

For your own benefit, it may be easier to choose a low balanced credit card or loan, one lets say has a balance that if you paid an extra $25.00 a week you would be able to see it being paid off within a six month to a year period of time. Remember, you must be consistent and not derailed from your goal.

If you do not do something to alleviate your debt, it will grow like weeds in the grass. Weeds always grow faster than the healthy plant life that you desire to grow. Debt is the same. It grows whether you feed it or not, once you have it in your budget it can take over. Do not allow yourself excuses, you must be determined to get out of debt.

Keep in mind, when you decide to climb your mountain of debt you are indeed climbing a mountain. It is done one step at a time, one cleft of rock to the next, reaching toward your goal to conquer the mountain.

Types of budget makers

As we learned earlier, there are obese, normal, bulimic and anorexic types of budgets. Let's examine each type in context of becoming debt free.

The OBESE Budget Maker

I want what I want and I want it now!

Like a person who has let their self go to obesity; unregulated spending, applying for all credit cards, consolidating debt to free up credit cards to turn around and return again to uncontrolled spending, once again find that they return to using credit fervently, a gross misconduct of finances, has created a never ending circle of self induced stress. This type of uncontrolled spending will lead to over indulgences.

Shakespeare in his play, Julius Caesar 1601, stated, "Cry havoc, and let slip the dogs of war!" In this simple play of Shakespeare, Julius Caesar is killed by his devoted general Anthony. Anthony then finds himself plagued throughout the play with the ghost or memory of Julius Caesar, following him about and never letting Anthony rest.

Shakespeare's play of constant plague of stepping beyond the boundaries is reflective of the budget that is overwhelmed with abuse. Only you can stop your spending. You can, "Cry havoc and let slip the dogs of war" finding yourself a conqueror and not a victim of over indulgences.

First let's look at what your current income is:

Income Source	Monthly Income
Job/Pension	
Alimony	
Social Security	
Spousal Income	
2nd Job	
Total	$

The ANOREXIC Budget Maker

If you are of the anorexic type budget, you have more than likely found every savings idea and you more than likely implement every technique into your budget.

Recently on Oprah the **Heinz family** was featured on her show. When she shopped for grocery her money savings were so astronomical that it truly was astounding. What wasn't revealed was the amount of time it required from her on a daily basis as well as weekly; in my budget time is money, in most cases of such a remarkable result as the Heinz family featured on Oprah, their savings extravaganza is a job or better yet a career. Now if you have more time than money then absolutely use your excess of time to pursue as much savings as you can. This is a great exercise for the unemployed or displaced worker, or anyone who finds themselves upside down and falling faster.

The BULIMIC Budget Maker

The Bulimic budget is commonly found among the population, as persons who feel as though they have, "earned" the right to go and have a good time or buy a new………. But regret it soon after they have purchased the item. Finding themselves racing back to the department store to return the item and then chastising them self for the over indulgence.

Realize that success to any budget is creating an allowance that can be spent. Making available finances that are allowed specifically for a .... Or a ...., will curb the need to gorge.

The BALANCED Budget Maker

The Balanced budget is one that really is able to absorb the rain of economic crisis, and perform well for its master. The person who rules their finances in general cannot be ruled by financial chaos. The Balanced budgeter pays their tithe, (gives to charity), pays themselves, and usually does not have a carry over balance of credit from month to month. Having a balanced budget takes discipline, being goal oriented, fixing their eyes, visualizing success in meeting the goals put before them.

Although I have no proof that a balanced budget will extend your life, it stands to reason that it could contribute to good health. There is less stress on the person who lives within a balanced budget. We all know that less stress is good for a healthy lifestyle. Reaching the goal, a balanced budget, is attainable; when you are working toward a balanced budget, you will reap many rewards, good health, peace of mind, fortitude and a sense of accomplishment.

Here are some easy get started tips when working through your goals.

(Important to write your goal(s) down and review them everyday, keep a quick view note in your wallet, on your mirror, or door, wherever your will see it daily.)

1)   Keep a journal to capture your thoughts and progress

2)   Review your progress to your goal weekly

 a) track your spending daily

 b) prepare for your day, take your own coffee, lunch etc

 c) check your account at the end of the week see that you are spending only what you have budgeted

 d) read your 30 day challenge out loud and keep up the good work

3)   Review with yourself and your spouse your progress over a 2 week period

a) track your daily and weekly spending

b) See yourself accomplishing your budget goals

c) Discuss your progress-make an extra minimum payment on any bill that you have on your primary goal list, with the money you have saved.

d) Read your 30 day challenge out loud and keep up the good work

4) Review your week

5) Review your month

6) Review your entire month with the help of your journal

7) See yourself gaining toward your goal

8) Add another 30 day challenge

9) Discuss your progress with yourself and your spouse-make an extra savings deposit from the finances you have saved from your diligence of saving money.

10) Repeat the process over the next three months

11) Journal yourself and your progress as you will have a tendency to forget the progress you **have** made.

By seeing the progress of your vision coming to pass it will inspire you to continue

12) Remind yourself of your goals-keep them in front of you

You are the key to your success or failure. It has been said the Author of the Universe did not make road; leading nowhere. Personally speaking, my God is in control and He has arranged my steps, however I know that He is also a Gentleman and will not interfere where He is not wanted. Therefore, my success is found when I cooperate with His teachings and follow them. Wisdom of finances is given, knowledge of how to handle finances is given, His faithfulness is given; all I must do to ensure that I receive His benefits is follow His path and directions from His Word.

"Ask and it shall be given unto you."

References

Statistics and other information contained in this book were compiled from the following sources:

www.uscourts.gov/bankruptcycourts.html

www.ftc.gov/bcp/edu/pubs/consumer/credit/cre41.sht m

www.msnbc.msn.com/

www.bankruptcyaction.com/

www.bankruptcyhome.com/

www.bankruptcyinformation.com/

www.fanniemae.com/index.jhtml

http://content.healthaffairs.org/cgi/content/abstract/h lthaff.w5.63v1

End Notes

Proceeds from the sale of this book are used to serve people in need, specifically those impacted by a disaster. We recognize that disasters come in different forms, yet all the storms in life are personal. Through Lifeline Ministries we seek to stand in the gap, meeting people where they are at, physically, emotionally and spiritually, to give them a hand up in the time of need.

By purchasing this book you are making an investment, not only in your own life, but in those in your inner circle and countless others, touching both hearts and lives.

Thank you.

www.ingramcontent.com/pod-product-compliance
Lightning Source LLC
Chambersburg PA
CBHW071225170526
45165CB00003B/990

*9 7 8 1 4 4 8 6 6 1 2 3 7 *